This book is dedicated to

Tim Roush,

who loved science and the Creator.

As an exemplary educator, his spirit of

creative storytelling inspired so many young learners

to reach for the stars. His life truly exemplified showing

us all how to take care of the Earth and each other

with love, humor, and humility.

We'll see you on the other side

of the stars, my friend!

Back in the beginning of time,

the part of time that we can only imagine,

the Creator carefully placed nine balls of dust

into the midst of the cosmos.

These cosmic "marbles" were all lined up

with one mighty star, the sun,

the source

of

light and life.

The first marble, the now-forgotten

planet to be called Pluto

was the farthest from the source.

As the Creator spoke life into the planet,

there were only two things that were asked of it.

The Creator said,

"I ONLY ASK THAT YOU TAKE CARE OF THIS PLANET

AND EACH OTHER."

Now, Pluto had the smallest of plans in mind,

as the smallest planet.

Its creatures had no goals

but to live for themselves.

They were so far away from the source

that they had no vision.

They forgot to do those things

they were asked to do!

They did not take care of their planet

or each other.

The Creator gave them all time to
decide how to live well together,
but instead they chose not to open their eyes;
to forever sleep
the frozen sleep of rock and ice.

The Creator then sighed and awoke

the next planet

to be called Neptune.

The Creator said,

"I ONLY ASK THAT YOU TAKE CARE OF THIS PLANET

AND EACH OTHER."

All of the fish and creatures of

the seas of Neptune

stirred with excitement!

Every last one of them were born to water,

but in the depths of their

deep, great oceans

they never longed to catch

the light of the sun.

They did not want to learn how to breathe

outside of their thick, soupy waters.

They did not want to swim together to stay safe,

so they too finally chose to sleep alone,

while only great winds lived on

to whip through the dark and cold seas!

The Creator looked again at the line of planets,

and once again opened up new hope.

Floating out in space like a giant helium balloon,

Uranus was given the chance to be something really

big!

Once again, the Creator said,

"I ONLY ASK THAT YOU TAKE CARE OF THIS PLANET

AND EACH OTHER.

With their 27 glorious moons, the creatures of this planet became full of themselves, thinking they were so much better than any other creation!

They argued and fought over
which way their moons should spin!
In all of their anger, they flipped over
the whole planet on its side,
and could not see the
source of light anymore!

All of its beauty was lost because
they could not come together
to live as they were asked.
It was doomed to be a lonely ice giant
few would ever see!

You might think that after three tries,

the Creator would just give up

and move onto a new galaxy!

Instead, the Creator awoke the planet Saturn,

and once again said,

**"I ONLY ASK THAT YOU TAKE CARE OF THIS PLANET
AND EACH OTHER."**

The creatures of Saturn thought

that they knew

exactly what they had to do

to make this happen.

They worked together to create some

82 moons and spectacular rings of seven!

They did as they were
told for a long time,
but they finally got tired
of sharing and caring,
and used up all of the things
that had helped them
to live together!

Once again,

the simple things that were

asked of them were ignored,

and the planet Saturn

could no longer support life.

Two more planets,

Jupiter and Mars

took on the promise of caring for

their planets

and for their creatures.

Two times more,

the promise was broken,

and ancient lands

were left as poison to the planets.

Even after all of these planets' mistakes,

the Creator made the same offer for the 7th time,

this time to the planet Earth.

Again, the Creator said,

"I ONLY ASK THAT YOU TAKE CARE OF THIS PLANET

AND EACH OTHER."

This time,

the Creator put human beings

in charge of the Earth and gave them control.

As humans took over,

the other creatures allowed them

to walk with them

on the planet.

The plants bloomed and spread,

to bring beauty and food

for the human beings

and the other creatures.

The animals also provided

food for the humans.

But, over time,

the humans started

to once again

forget their source of light and life.

They took too much good

from the land,

and put too much bad into

the air and water.

The bad air started to block the sun and

poison the food

that would keep them well.

They forgot to take care of one another

and took as much as they could

for themselves.

Wars were fought, people got sick.

Then, as they started to slip into sadness,

one by one, people awoke

and started listening again to the earth.

The more people listened,

the more they planted what the Earth needed.

The more they planted what was needed,

the healthier the planet got!

The healthier the planet got,

the more humans wanted

to take care of one another!

One by one,
each person learned to
keep the promise to….

"….TAKE CARE OF THIS PLANET AND EACH OTHER."